THE BEATLES
SONGS WITH JUST 3 OR 4 CHORDS

Photo © Apple Corps Limited

ISBN 978-1-5400-2660-6

HAL•LEONARD®

Visit Hal Leonard Online at
www.halleonard.com

Contact Us:
Hal Leonard
7777 West Bluemound Road
Milwaukee, WI 53213
Email: info@halleonard.com

In Europe contact:
Hal Leonard Europe Limited
Distribution Centre, Newmarket Road
Bury St Edmunds, Suffolk, IP33 3YB
Email: info@halleonard

In Australia contact:
Hal Leonard Australia Pty. Ltd.
4 Lentara Court
Cheltenham, Victoria, 3192 Australia
Email: info@halleonard.com.au

CONTENTS

Act Naturally

Words and Music by
Vonie Morrison and Johnny Russell

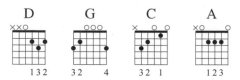

Intro
| D | | G | ‖

Verse 1
G | | C | |
They're gonna put me in the movies;
G | | D |
They're gonna make a big star out of me.
|G | | C |
We'll make a film about a man that's sad and lonely,
|D | | G | N.C.
And all I gotta do is   act natural - ly.

Bridge 1
‖D | | G |
Well, I bet you I'm gonna be a big star.
|D | | G |
Might win an Oscar; you can't never tell.
|D | | G |
The movies gonna make me a big star,
|A | | D |
'Cause I can play the part so well.

Verse 2

‖ **G** | | **C** | |

Well, I hope you come and see me in the movies,

G | | **D** |

Then I'll know that you will plainly see

| **G** | | **C** |

The biggest fool that ever hit the big time,

| **D** | | **G** | **N.C.** ‖

And all I gotta do is   act natural - ly.

Interlude

| **D** | | **G** | |

| **D** | | **G** |

Verse 3

‖ **G** | | **C** |

We'll make the scene about a man that's sad and lonely

| **G** | | **D** |

And beggin' down up - on his bended knee.

| **G** | | **C** |

I'll play the part and I won't need re - hearsin',

D | | **G** | **N.C.**

All I have to do is   act natural - ly.

Bridge 2   *Repeat Bridge 1*

Verse 4   *Repeat Verse 2*

Outro | **D** | | **G** | ‖

Beautiful Dreamer

Words and Music by Stephen Foster
New Words and Music by
Gerry Goffin and Jack Keller

G   C   D   A

Verse 1

G | |C | |
Beautiful dream - er, come on, baby, wake up to me.

D | | |G ||
Can't you see me, ba - by? I'm a down on bended knee.

Verse 2

G | |C | |
Beautiful dream - er, come on, baby, hear me one time.

D | | |G ||
I'll give you the world, ___ baby, if you'll ___ just say you'll be mine.

Bridge 1

D | |G | |
I used to dream of Jeannie with the light brown hair.

A | |D N.C. | ||
Since I met you, baby, that girl ain't anywhere.

Verse 3

G | |C | |
Beautiful dream - er, come on and end my misery.

D | | |G ||
Oh, beautiful dream - er, won't you ___ wake up to me?

Guitar Solo

|G | |C | |
|D | | |G ||

Bridge 2

Repeat Bridge 1

Verse 4

Repeat Verse 3

Verse 5

G | |C | |
Beautiful dream - er, wake up to me.

D | | |G ||
Beautiful dream - er, I'm on bended knee.

Outro-Verse

G | |C | |
Beautiful dream - er, wake up to me.

D | | |G C |G ||
Beautiful dream - er, I'm on bended knee, ___ oh, yeah.

Get Back

Words and Music by
John Lennon and Paul McCartney

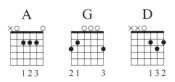

Intro |A | | | G D ‖

Verse 1

A | |
Jo-Jo was a man who thought ___ he was a loner,
       |D |A
But ___ he knew it couldn't last.
       | |
Jo-Jo left his home in Tuc - son, Arizona
       |D |A
For ___ some California grass.

Chorus 1

              ‖A |
Get back, ___   get back,
       |D |A   G
Get back ___ to where you once belonged.
   D |A |
Get back, ___   get back,
       |D |A
Get back ___ to where you once belonged.
              ‖
Get back, Jo-Jo.

Interlude 1

```
|A          |          |D         |A    G D |
|A          |          |D         |A    G
```

Chorus 2

```
      D      ‖A                      |
Go back, ___           get back,
                |D                       |A    G
Get back ___ to where you once belonged.
      D      |A                      |
Get back, ___           get back,
             |                   C    D    |
Get back      to where you once be - longed ___
             |              ‖
Yeah.      Oo, get back, Jo!
```

Interlude 2

```
‖: A        |          |D         |A    G D :‖
```

Verse 2

```
A                              |
Sweet Loretta Martin thought ___ she was a woman,
   |D                      |A
But ___ she was another man.
      |                   |
All ___ the girls around her say ___ she's got it coming
      |D                   |A    G
But ___ she gets it while she can.
```

Chorus 3

```
      D      ‖A                      |
Oh, get back, ___           get back,
      |D                        |A    G
Get back ___ to where you once belonged.
   D      |A                      |
Get back, ___           get back,
      |D                        |A
Get back ___ to where you once belonged.
                |
Get back, Loretta.
```

| *Interlude 3* | |A | |D |A   G D | |
| | |A | |D |A   G |

            D   ‖**A** |

Chorus 4   Oh, get back, ___   get back,

                          |**D** | **G**

Get back ___ to where you once belonged.

            D |**A** |

Oh, get back, ___   get back.

                      |**D** | ‖

Get back ___ to where you once belonged.   Oo.

            A | |**D**

Interlude 4   *Oo,   ow!   Get back, Loretta,*

                            |**A**   **G D**

Your mama's waitin' for you,

                     |**A** |

Wearin' her high-heel shoes

                              |**D**

And her low-neck sweater.

                   |**A**   **G**

Get back home, Loretta.

            D   ‖**A** |

Outro-Chorus Get back, ___   get back,

                      |**D** |**A** **G**

Get back ___ to where you once belonged.

            D |**A** |

Oh, get back, ___   get back,

                      |**D** |**A**   ‖

Get back, ___   oh, yeah.

Come Together

Words and Music by
John Lennon and Paul McCartney

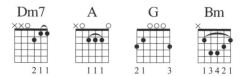

Intro

‖:**Dm7** | :‖
(Shoot me.)   (Shoot me.)

Verse 1

Dm7 |
  Here come old flat top, he come grooving up slowly,

| |
He got joo joo eyeball, he one holy roller,

|**A** | |
He got hair down to his knees,

G **N.C.** | |
Got to be a joker, he just do what he please.

|**Dm7** | | | ‖

Verse 2

Dm7 |
  He wear no shoe shine, he got toe jam football,

| |
He got monkey finger, he shoot Coca Cola,

|**A** | |
He say, "I know you, you know me.

G **N.C.** |
One thing I can tell you is you got to be free."

Chorus 1

‖**Bm**
Come togeth - er,

A |**G** **A** **N.C.**
Right   now,

|**Dm7** | | | ‖
Over me.

Verse 3

Dm7 |

  He bag production, he got walrus gumboot,

           | |

He got Ono sideboard, he one spinal cracker,

       |A | |

He got   feet down below his knee,

G   N.C. |

Hold you in his armchair, you can feel his disease.

Chorus 2

                      ‖ Bm

Come togeth - er,

A |G   A N.C.

Right   now,

        |Dm7 | ‖

Over me.   Right!

Solo

|Dm7 | | |

|A | | |Dm7 | ‖

Verse 4

Dm7 |

  He roller coaster, he got early warning,

         | |

He got muddy water, he one mojo filter,

      |A | |

He say, "One and one and one is three."

G N.C. |

Got to be good looking 'cause he's so hard to see.

Chorus 3

                      ‖ Bm

Come togeth - er,

A |G   A N.C.

Right   now,

        ‖ Dm7 | | | ‖

Over me.   Oh!

|Dm7 | ‖: | :‖

Outro

                        Come together, yeah!   *Repeat and fade*

Don't Let Me Down

Words and Music by
John Lennon and Paul McCartney

Intro

|E |

Chorus 1

‖F♯m |
Don't let me down.
|E |
Don't let me down.
|F♯m |
Don't let me down,
|E |
Don't let me down.

Verse 1

‖F♯m
Nobody ever loved me like she does,
| |E |
Ooh, she does, yes she does,
|F♯m
And if somebody loved me like she do me,
| |E |
Ooh, she do me, yes she does.

Chorus 2

Repeat Chorus 1

Bridge

         ‖ **E** |

I'm in love for the first time,

           | **B7** |

Don't you know it's going to last.

          | |

It's a love that lasts forev - er,

       | **E** |

It's a love that has no   past.

Chorus 3   *Repeat Chorus 1*

Verse 2

                                ‖ **F♯m**

And from the first time that she really done me,

     | | **E** |

Ooh, she done me, she done me good.

       | **F♯m**

I guess nobody ever really done me,

     | | **E** |

Ooh, she done me, she done me good.

Chorus 4

         ‖ **F♯m** |

Don't let me down, hey!

      | **E** |

Don't let me down.

      | **F♯m** |

Don't let me down,

       | **E** | |

Don't let me down.

F♯m | **E**

  Don't let me down,

     | **F♯m** |

Don't let me down.

Can you dig it?

     | **E** | ‖

Don't let me down.

Don't Pass Me By

Words and Music by
Richard Starkey

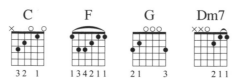

Intro

|C |

Verse 1

‖C | |
I listen for your footsteps coming up the drive,
F | |
Listen for your footsteps, but they don't arrive.
G |
Waiting for your knock, dear, on my old front door,
     |F
I don't hear it,
                         | |C |
Does it mean you don't love me any - more?

Verse 2

‖C | |
I hear the clock a ticking on the mantel shelf,
F |
See the hands a moving, but I'm by myself.
 |G |
I wonder where you are tonight and why I'm by myself,
       |F
I don't see you,
                         | |C |
Does it mean you don't love me any - more?

Chorus 1

‖ C
Don't pass me by, don't make me cry,

|
Don't make me blue,

| F |
'Cause you know, darling, I love only you.

| C |
You'll never know it hurt me so, I'll hate to see you go,

| G |
Don't pass me by,

| F | | C |
Don't make me cry.

Verse 3

‖ C | ` |
I'm sorry that I doubted you, I was so unfair,

F |
You were in a car crash and you lost your hair.

| G |
You said that you would be late, a - bout an hour or two,

| F
I say that's alright,

| | C |
I'm waiting here, just waiting to hear from you.

Chorus 2

‖ C
Don't pass me by, don't make me cry,

|
Don't make me blue,

| F |
'Cause you know, darling, I love only you.

| C |
You'll never know it hurt me so, I'll hate to see you go,

| G |
Don't pass me by,

| F | ‖
Don't make me cry.

Interlude | C | | N.C. | ` | C |

Chorus 3   *Repeat Chorus 2*

Outro | C | | F | G | Dm7   C | N.C. | | ‖ *Fade out*

15

Eleanor Rigby

Words and Music by
John Lennon and Paul McCartney

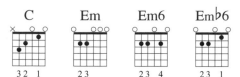

Intro

C | |**Em** | |
Ah, look at all the lonely peo - ple!
C | |**Em** | ||
Ah, look at all the lonely peo - ple!

Verse 1

Em |
Eleanor Rigby,

                | |**C** |
Picks up the rice in the church where a wedding has been,
       Em |
Lives in a dream.

             |
Waits at the window,

              | |**C** |
Wearing a face that she keeps in a jar by the door,
       Em ||
Who is it for?

Chorus 1

Em |**Em6** |**Em♭6** |**Em** |
All the lonely people, where do they all come from?
        |**Em6** |**Em♭6** |**Em** ||
All the lonely people, where do they all be - long?

Verse 2

    Em |
Father McKenzie,

               | |**C**
Writing the words of a ser - mon that no one will hear,

    | **Em** |
No one comes near.

               |
Look at him working,

               | |**C** |
Darning his socks in the night when there's nobody there,

          Em   ‖
What does he care?

Chorus 2   *Repeat Chorus 1*

Bridge

C | |**Em** | |
Ah, look at all the lonely peo - ple!
C | |**Em** | ‖
Ah, look at all the lonely peo - ple!

Verse 3

    Em |
Eleanor Rigby,

               | |**C** |
Died in the church and was bur - ied along with her name,

        Em |
Nobody came.

               |
Father McKenzie,

               | |**C** |
Wiping the dirt from his hands as he walks from the grave,

        Em   ‖
No one was saved.

Chorus 3   *Repeat Chorus 1*

Helter Skelter

Words and Music by
John Lennon and Paul McCartney

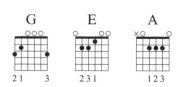

Intro | N.C.

Verse 1
‖N.C.
When I   get to the bottom I go back to the top of the slide,

Where I stop and turn and I go for a ride,
                                                                |G
Till I get to the bottom, and I see you a - gain,
                    |E   ‖
Yeah, yeah, yeah!

Verse 2
E
Do you, don't you want me to love you?

I'm coming down fast, but I'm miles above you.

Tell me, tell me, tell me,
              |G
Come on, tell me the answer.
          |A |E   ‖
Well, you may be a lover, but you ain't no danc - er.

Chorus 1
A |E |
Helter Skelter, Helter Skelter.
|A |E | | ‖
Helter Skelter, yeah!

Verse 3
E
Will you, won't you want me to make you?

I'm coming down fast, but don't let me break you.
G
Tell me, tell me, tell me the answer.
      |A |E
You may be a lover, but you ain't no danc - er.
          ‖
Look out!

Chorus 2

A |E |
Helter Skelter, Helter Skelter.
A |E |
Helter Skelter,   Oo!

                     | ‖
Look out 'cause here she comes!

Guitar Solo

|A |E |A |E

Verse 4

Repeat Verse 1

Verse 5

E |
Well, do you, don't you want me to make you?
       | | |
I'm coming down fast, but don't let me break you.
G
Tell me, tell me, tell me your answer.
       |A |E
Well, you may be a lover, but you ain't no danc - er,
       ‖
Look out!

Chorus 3

A |E |
Helter Skelter, Helter Skelter.
A |E
Helter Skelter.
      |
Look out! Helter Skelter!
     | |
She's coming down fast!
     | |
Yes she is, yes she is
         ‖
Coming down fast.

Outro

‖:E | :‖ *Repeat and fade*

Honey Don't

Words and Music by
Carl Lee Perkins

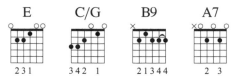

Intro

|N.C. | |E | |

Verse 1

‖E | |C/G
Well, how come you say you will ___ when you won't?
                              | |E
Say you do, baby, when you don't?
                              | |C/G
Let me know, honey, how you feel.
                              |
Tell the truth now, is love real?
       |B9 | |E |
But ah, ___ hah,   well, honey, don't.

Chorus 1

‖E | | |
Well, honey, don't.   Honey, don't.
              |A7 | |E |
Honey, don't.   Honey, don't.
       |B9
I say you will when you won't,
       | |E |
Ah, ___ hah, honey, don't.

Verse 2

             ‖E | |C/G
Well, I love ___ you, baby and you ought ___ to know

               |
I like the way that you wear yer clothes.

  |E |
Ev - 'rything about you is so doggone sweet.

   |C/G |
You got that sand all over your feet.

        |B9 | |E |
But ah, ___ hah,   well, honey, don't.

Chorus 2

               ‖E | | |
Honey, don't.   Honey, don't.

              |A7 | |E |
Honey, don't.   Honey, don't.

        |B9
I say you will when you won't,

   | |E | ‖
Ah, ___ hah, honey, don't.

Guitar Solo 1

|E		|C/G		
|E		|C/G	|B9	
|E					
|A7		|E		
|B9		|E	

Verse 3

```
             ‖E                        |           |C/G
```
Well, sometimes I love you on a Saturday night.
```
                              |              |E
```
Sunday morning you don't ___ look right.
```
                              |           |
```
You've been out paint - in' the town.
```
C/G                |
```
Ah, ha, baby, been steppin' around.
```
        |B9              |              |E
```
But, ah, ___ hah, well, ___ honey, don't.

Chorus 3

```
              |          ‖E          |              |              |
```
I said, ___ honey, don't.   Honey, don't.
```
                    |A7          |              |E          |
```
Honey, don't.   Honey, don't.
```
                    |B9
```
I say you will when you won't,
```
              |                    |E          |              ‖
```
Ah, ___ hah, honey, don't.

Guitar Solo 2

```
| E        |          | C/G        |          |
| E        |          | C/G        | B9        ‖
```


Outro-Chorus

```
        E          |                    |          |
```
Well, honey, don't.
```
                    |A7              |
```
Well, honey, don't.
```
                    |E          |
```
A little, little honey don't.
```
              |B9
```
I say you will when you won't,
```
              |              |E          |          ‖
```
Ah, ___ hah, honey, don't.

Let It Be

Words and Music by
John Lennon and Paul McCartney

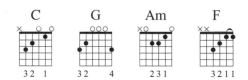

Intro |C   G |Am   F |C   G |F   C

Verse 1
‖C   G |
When I find myself in times of trouble
Am   F |
Mother Mary comes to me
C   G
Speaking words of wis - dom,
   |F   C
Let it be.
   | G
And in my hour of dark - ness
   |Am   F |
She is standing right in front of me
C   G
Speaking words of wisdom,
   |F   C
Let it be.

Chorus 1
     ‖Am   G
Let it be, __ let it be,
          |F   C |
Ah, let it be, __ let it be.
             G
Whisper words of wisdom,
   |F   C
Let it be.

Verse 2

```
        ‖C                      G           |
And when the broken heart - ed people
Am                    F           |
Living in the world __ agree,
C                     G
There will be an an - swer,
      |F     C
Let it be.
      |                  G             |
For though they may be part - ed there is
Am                    F             |
Still a chance that they __ will see
C                     G
There will be an an - swer,
      |F        C
Let it be.
```

Chorus 2

```
         ‖Am         G
Let it be, __ let it be,
         |F           C   |
Ah, let it be, __ let it be.
                      G
 Yeah, there will be an an - swer,
      |F     C
Let it be.
```

Chorus 3   *Repeat Chorus 1*

Interlude |F   C |G   F   C |F   C |G   F   C ‖

Guitar Solo |C   G |Am   F |C   G |F   C |
                      | G |Am   F |C   G |F   C

Chorus 4   *Repeat Chorus 1*

Verse 3

```
     ‖ C                    G
And when the night is cloud - y
       | Am            F              |
There is still a light that shines on me;
C              G
Shine until tomor - row,
     | F    C
Let it be.
     |                     G              |
I wake up to the sound __ of music;
Am                    F            |
Mother Mary comes __ to me,
C                 G
Speaking words of wisdom,
       | F      C
Let it be.
```

Chorus 5

```
          ‖ Am           G
Let it be, __ let it be,
                   | F          C
Ah, let it be, __ let it be.
          |                 G
Yeah, there will be an an - swer,
       | F    C
Let it be.
          | Am           G
Let it be, __ let it be,
                   | F          C    |
Ah, let it be, __ let it be.
                        G
Whisper words of wisdom,
       | F    C    ‖
Let it be.
```

Outro

```
| F    C  | G   F   C  ‖
```

I Saw Her Standing There

Words and Music by
John Lennon and Paul McCartney

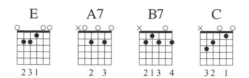

Intro

N.C. |**E** | | |
One, two, three, four!

Verse 1

      ‖**E** |
Well, she was just seventeen,
 |**A7** |**E**
You know what I mean,
   | | |**B7** |
And the way she looked was way beyond com - pare.
 |**E** | |**A7** |**C**
So how could I dance with anoth - er, woo,
  |**E** |**B7** |**E** |
When I saw her standing there?

Verse 2

      ‖**E** |
Well, she looked at me,
  |**A7** |**E**
And I, I could see
  | | |**B7** | |
That be - fore too long I'd fall in love with her.
E | |**A7** |**C**
She wouldn't dance with anoth - er, woo,
  |**E** |**B7** |**E** |
When I saw her standing there.

Bridge 1

```
        ‖ A7              |
Well, my heart went boom

        |                 |
When I crossed that room

        |         |   | B7       |          | A7        |
And I held her hand  in  mine.
```

Verse 3

```
                ‖ E                    |
Oh, we danced    through the night,

         | A7                  | E
And we held each other tight,

         |          |          | B7       |
And be - fore too long I fell in love with her.

       | E        |          | A7      | C
Now I'll never dance with anoth - er,   woo,

       | E      | B7        | E      |        ‖
Since I saw  her  standing there.
```

Interlude

```
| E          |          |          |          |
|          |          | B7       |          |
| E          |          | A7       |          |
| E          | B7        | E        |
```

Bridge 2

Repeat Bridge 1

Verse 4

```
                ‖ E                    |
Oh, we danced    through the night,

         | A7                  | E
And we held each other tight,

         |          |          | B7       |
And be - fore too long I fell in love with her.

       | E        |          | A7      | C
Now I'll never dance with anoth - er,   woo,

       | E      | B7        | E      |
Since I saw  her  standing there.

         |        | B7          | E        |
Oh, since I saw  her standing there.

                | B7          | A7     | E      |        ‖
Yeah, well, since I saw  her standing there.
```

I've Just Seen a Face

Words and Music by
John Lennon and Paul McCartney

(Capo 2nd fret)

Em   C   D   G

Intro

|**Em** | | | |

|**C** | | | |**D** |**C** ||

Verse 1

G |
I've just seen a face

         | | |**Em**
I can't for - get the time or place where we just met.

        |
She's just the girl for me

     | | |**C** |
And I want all the world to see we've met.

      |**D** |**G** ||
Mm mm mm mm mm.

Verse 2

G |
Had it been an - other day

| |
I might have looked the other way

  |**Em** |
And I'd have never been aware.

    | | |**C** |
But as it is I'll dream of her tonight,

    |**D** |**G** ||
Da da da da da da.

Chorus 1

D |
Falling,

       |C |
Yes, I am falling,

         |G |
And she keeps calling

C |G | ||
  Me back a - gain.

Verse 3

G | |
I have never known the like of this;

      | |
I've been a - lone and I have

Em |
Missed things and kept out of sight.

   | | |C |
But other girls were never quite like this,

    |D |G ||
Da da da da da da.

Chorus 2   *Repeat Chorus 1*

Interlude |G | | | |Em | |

          | | |C | |D |C ||

Chorus 3   *Repeat Chorus 1*

Verse 4   *Repeat Verse 1*

Chorus 4   *Repeat Chorus 1 (2x)*

Outro-Chorus

D |
Oh, falling,

       |C |
Yes, I am falling,

         |G |
And she keeps calling

C | |D |G ||
  Me back a - gain.

Love Me Do

Words and Music by
John Lennon and Paul McCartney

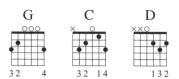

Intro

|G |C |G |C |

|G |C |G | ||

Chorus 1

G |C
Love, love me do.

  |G |C
You know I love you.

  |G |C
I'll always be true.

  | | | N.C.
So please,

    |G |C |G |C ||
Love me do.   Oh, love me do.

Chorus 2

G |C
 Love, love me do.

  |G |C
You know I love you.

  |G |C
I'll always be true.

  | | | N.C.
So please,

    |G |C |G | ||
Love me do.   Oh, love me do.

Bridge

D | |
Someone to love,
C |**G** |
Somebody new.
D | |
Someone to love,
C |**G** ‖
Someone like you.

Chorus 3 *Repeat Chorus 1*

Harmonica Solo ‖: **D** | |**C** |**G** :‖
| | | | **D** ‖

Chorus 4

G |**C**
Love, love me do.
|**G** |**C**
You know I love you.
|**G** |**C**
I'll always be true.
| | | **N.C.**
So please,
|**G** |**C** |**G** |**C**
Love me do.   Oh, love me do.
‖: **G** |**C**
Yeah, love me do.
|**G** |**C** :‖
Oh, love me do. Yeah,   ***Repeat and fade***

31

Mean Mr. Mustard

Words and Music by
John Lennon and Paul McCartney

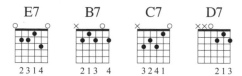

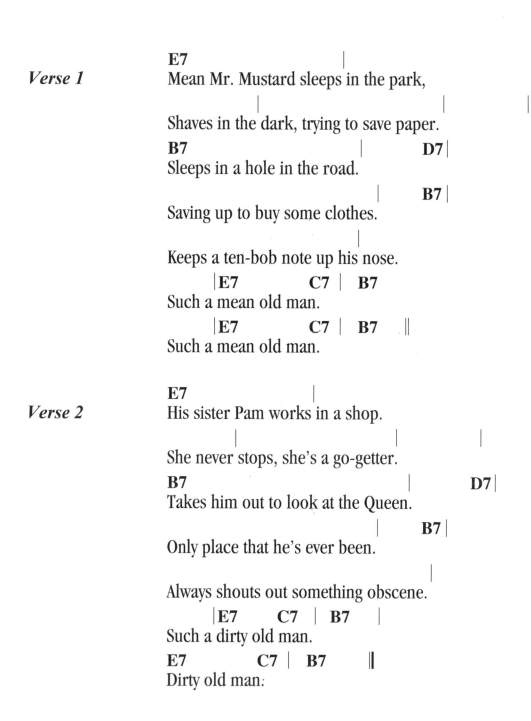

Verse 1

E7
Mean Mr. Mustard sleeps in the park,

Shaves in the dark, trying to save paper.

B7   **D7**
Sleeps in a hole in the road.

                    B7
Saving up to buy some clothes.

Keeps a ten-bob note up his nose.

|**E7**   **C7** | **B7**
Such a mean old man.

|**E7**   **C7** | **B7**   ‖
Such a mean old man.

Verse 2

E7
His sister Pam works in a shop.

She never stops, she's a go-getter.

B7   **D7**
Takes him out to look at the Queen.

                    B7
Only place that he's ever been.

Always shouts out something obscene.

|**E7**   **C7** | **B7**
Such a dirty old man.

E7   **C7** | **B7**   ‖
Dirty old man:

Why Don't We Do It in the Road

Words and Music by
John Lennon and Paul McCartney

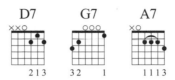

Intro
```
|N.C.    |        |        |
```

Verse 1

N.C.   ‖D7 |
Why don't we do it in the road?

                              | |
Why don't we do it in the road?

                              |G7 |
Why don't we do it in the road?

                              |D7 | |
Why don't we do it in the road?

A7
No one will be watching us.

  |G7 |D7 |
Why ___ don't we do it in the road?

Verse 2   *Repeat Verse 1*

Verse 3

N.C.   ‖D7 |
Why don't we do it in the road?

                              | |
Why don't we do it in the road?

                              |G7 |
Why don't we do it in the road?

                              |D7 | |
Why don't we do it in the road?

A7 |G7
No one will be watching us.

N.C. |D7 N.C. ‖
Why don't we do it in the road?

Ob-La-Di, Ob-La-Da

Words and Music by
John Lennon and Paul McCartney

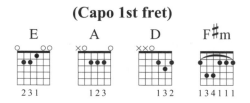

(Capo 1st fret)

Intro

|E |A | | | ||

Verse 1

A |E |
Desmond has a barrow in the market place,
                              |A |
Molly is the singer in a band.
                                        |D
Desmond says to Molly, girl, I like your face,
          |A   E |A
And Molly says this as she takes him by the hand.

Chorus 1

          ||A |E F♯m |
Ob-la-di, ob-la-da, life goes on, bra,
A   E |A
La, la, how their life goes on.
          | |E F♯m |
Ob-la-di, ob-la-da, life goes on, bra,
A |E |A ||
La, la, how their life goes on.

Verse 2

A |E |
Desmond takes a trolley to the jeweler's store,
                              |A |
Buys a twenty carat golden ring.
                                        |D
Takes it back to Molly waiting at the door,
          |A   E |A
And as he gives it to her, she begins to sing:

Chorus 2

Repeat Chorus 1

Bridge 1

D
  In a couple of years,
     | |A | |
They have built a home sweet home.
D |
  With a couple of kids running in the yard
 |A |E ||
Of Desmond and Molly Jones.

Verse 3

A |E |
Happy ever after in the market place,
                               |A |
Desmond lets the children lend a hand.
                                |D
Molly stays at home and does her pretty face,
          |A   E |A
And in the evening she still sings it with the band.

Chorus 3   *Repeat Chorus 1*

Bridge 2   *Repeat Bridge 1*

Verse 4

A |E |
Happy ever after in the market place,
                               |A |
Molly lets the children lend a hand.
                                |D
Desmond stays at home and does his pretty face,
          |A   E |A
And in the evening she's a singer with the band.

Chorus 4

           ||A |E F#m |
Ob-la-di, ob-la-da, life goes on, bra,
A   E |A
La, la, how their life goes on.
                 | |E F#m |
Ob-la-di, ob-la-da, life goes on, bra,
A |E |F#m
La, la, how their life goes on.
           |
And if you want some fun,
   |E   A ||
Take ob-la-di-bla-da.

Octopus's Garden

Words and Music by
Richard Starkey

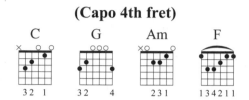

(Capo 4th fret)

C   G   Am   F

Intro

| N.C. | G   C N.C. | | |
| C | Am | F | G   ‖

Verse 1

C | |
   I'd like to be

Am |
   Under the sea,

     | F | | G | |
In an octopus's garden in the shade.

C | |
   He'd let us in,

Am |
   Knows where we've been,

     | F | | G | |
In his octopus's garden in the shade.

Am | | | |
   I'd ask my friends to come and see

F | G | ‖
   An octo - pus's garden with me.

Chorus 1

C | |
   I'd like to be

Am |
   Under the sea

     | F | G | C | ‖
In an octopus's garden in the shade.

Verse 2

```
C              |              |
  We would be warm
Am             |
  Below the storm
     |F          |            |G       |          |
In our little hideaway beneath the waves.
C              |         |
  Resting our head
Am             |
  On the sea bed
    |F          |            |G        |          |
In an octopus's garden near a cave.
Am             |          |          |          |
  We would sing and dance around,
F              |          |G         |N.C.       ||
  Because we know we can't be found.
```

Chorus 2   *Repeat Chorus 1*

Verse 3

```
C              |              |
  We would shout
Am                 |
  And swim about
    |F          |            |G        |          |
The coral that lies beneath the waves.
C              |
  Oh, what joy
    |Am          |          |
For every girl and boy,
F              |          |G         |          |
Knowing they're happy and they're safe.
Am             |          |          |          |
  We would be so happy, you and me.
F              |          |G         |          ||
No one there to tell us what to do.
```

Chorus 3

```
C              |          |
  I'd like to be
Am             |
  Under the sea
     |F         |G        |Am        |
In an octopus's garden with you.
     |F         |G        |Am        |
In an octopus's garden with you.
     |F         |G        |C   N.C.      |   G   C   ||
In an octopus's garden with you.
```

Paperback Writer

Words and Music by
John Lennon and Paul McCartney

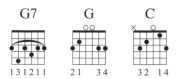

Intro

N.C. | | | |
Paperback writer... writer... writer.
|**G7** | | | |

Verse 1

‖**G** |
Dear Sir or Madam, will you read my book?

              | |
It took me years to write, will you take a look?

  | |
It's based on a novel by a man named Lear,

    |
And I need a job,

         | |**C** |
So I want to be a paperback writer,

            |**G** |
Paperback writer.

Verse 2

‖**G** |
It's a dirty story of a dirty man,

         | |
And his clinging wife doesn't understand.

  | |
His son is working for the Daily Mail.

    |
It's a steady job,

      | |**C** |
But he wants to be a paperback writer,

            |**G** | ‖
Paperback writer.

Interlude 1

N.C. | | | |
Paperback writer... writer... writer.
|G7 | | |

Verse 3

‖G |
It's a thousand pages, give or take a few.

   | |
I'll be writing more in a week or two.

   | |
I can make it longer if you like the style,

   |
I can change it 'round,

   | |C |
And I want to be a paperback writer,

       |G |
Paperback writer.

Verse 4

‖G |
If you really like it, you can have the rights.

   | |
It could make a million for you overnight.

   | |
If you must return it, you can send it here.

   |
But I need a break,

   | |C |
And I want to be a paperback writer,

       |G | ‖
Paperback writer.

Interlude 2

N.C. | | | |
Paperback writer... writer... writer.
|G7 | | | ‖

Outro

‖: G | | | :‖
   Paperback writer, paperback writer.   ***Repeat and fade***

Rain

Words and Music by
John Lennon and Paul McCartney

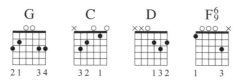

Intro |G | | |

Verse 1
‖G
If the rain comes,
         |C   D |G
They run and hide their heads.
         |C   D |G
They might as well be ___ dead,
         |C |
If the rain comes,
         |G |
If the rain ___ comes.

Verse 2
         ‖G
When the sun shines,
         |C   D |G
They slip in - to the shade,
         |C   D |G
And sip their lemon - ade,
                    |C |
When the sun shines, ___
                    |G | ‖
When the sun ___ shines.

Chorus 1

```
     G    |      |F♯6/9 |
Rain, _____
           |G     |      |
I don't mind.
           |      |F♯6/9 |
Shine, _____
                |G    |
The weather's fine.
```

Verse 3

```
          ‖G
I can show you
          |C      D      |G      |
That when it starts to rain,
C        D           |G
Every - thing's the same.
          |C         |
I can show you,
          |G         |          ‖
I can show you.
```

Chorus 2   *Repeat Chorus 1*

Verse 4

```
          ‖G
Can you hear me
          |C      D       |G
That when it rains and ___ shines ,
          |C    D    |G
It's just a state of mind?
             |C          |
Can you hear me?
             |G  |       ‖
Can you hear me?
```

Outro   ‖:G | | | :‖ *Repeat and fade*

Rocky Raccoon

Words and Music by
John Lennon and Paul McCartney

Am7   D7   G7   C

Intro

| Am7 |

Verse 1

‖ Am7
Now somewhere in the black mountain hills of Dakota,
| D7 |
There lived a young boy named Rocky Raccoon
G7 | C
    And one day his woman ran off with an - other guy.
                          | Am7
Hit young Rocky in the eye.

Rocky didn't like that,
          | D7
He said, "I'm gonna get that boy."
    | G7
So one day he walked into town,
                              | C   ‖
Booked himself a room in the local saloon.

Verse 2

Am7 | D7 |
Rocky Raccoon checked into his room,
G7 | C |
Only to find Gideon's Bi - ble.
Am7 | D7
Rocky had come, e - quipped with a gun,
   | G7 | C
To shoot off the legs of his ri - val.
    | Am7 | D7
His rival, it seems, had broken his dreams,
   | G7 | C
By stealing the girl of his fan - cy.
    | Am7 | D7
Her name was Magill, and she called herself Lil,
   | G7 | C
But everyone knew her as Nan - cy. ·

Verse 3

    ‖**Am7** |**D7**
Now she and her man, who called himself Dan,
    |**G7** |**C** |
Were in the next room at the hoe - down.
Am7 |**D7**
Rocky burst in, and grinning a grin,
      |**G7** |**C**
He said, "Danny boy, this is a show - down."
      |**Am7** |**D7**
But Daniel was hot, he drew first and shot,
      |**G7** |**C**   ‖
And Rocky collapsed in the cor - ner.

Piano Solo   ‖:**Am7** |**D7** |**G7** |**C**   :‖

Verse 4

    ‖**Am7** |**D7**
Now, the doctor came in, stinking of gin,
      |**G7** |**C**
And pro - ceeded to lie on the ta - ble.
      |**Am7**
He said, "Rocky, you met your match,"
      |**D7**
And Rocky said, "Doc, it's only a scratch,
      |**G7**
And I'll be better, I'll be better, Doc,
            |**C**
As soon as I am   able."

Verse 5

    ‖**Am7** |**D7** |
Now Rocky Raccoon, he fell back in his room,
G7 |**C** |
Only to find Gideon's Bi - ble.
Am7 |**D7**
Gideon checked out and left it, no doubt,
    |**G7** |**C**   ‖
To help with good Rocky's revival.

Outro-Piano Solo |**Am7** |**D7** |**G7** |**C** |
                          |**Am7** |**D7** |
                           (Come on, Rocky boy.)   (Come on, Rocky boy.)
                           |**G7** |**C**   **G7 C** ‖

She Said She Said

Words and Music by
John Lennon and Paul McCartney

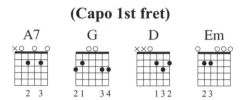

Intro |A7 | ||

Verse 1

A7   G |D
She said,

            |A7   G |D
"I know what it's like to be dead.

          |A7   G |D
I know what it is to be sad."

          |A7   G |D   A7 |
And she's making me feel like I've never been born.

| G |D   A7 ||

Verse 2

A7   G |D
I said,

           |A7   G |D
"Who put all those things in your head?

            |A7   G |D
Things that make me feel that I'm mad,

         |A7   G |D   A7 |
And you're making me feel like I've never been born."

| G |D   A7 ||

Bridge 1

A7   G |A7
She said, "You don't under - stand what I said."
      |G |A7
I said, "No, no, no, you're wrong.
             |Em |A7 |
When I was a boy
                |D |A7 |
Everything was right,
                |D ||
Everything was right."

Verse 3

A7   G |D
I said,
               |A7   G |D
"Even though you know what you know,
               |A7   G |D
I know that I'm ready to leave,
           |A7   G |D   A7 |
'Cause you're making me feel like I've never been born."
| G |D A7 ||

Bridge 2   *Repeat Bridge 1*

Verse 4   *Repeat Verse 3*

Outro

A7 |
She said, (She said.)
       |
"I know what it's like to be dead."
       |
(I know what it's like to be dead.)
       |
"I know what it is to be sad."
       |
(I know what it is to be sad.)
       | ||
"I know what it's like to be dead."   ***Fade out***

Slow Down

Words and Music by
Larry Williams

C   F   G

32 1   1 3 4 2 1 1   2 1   3 4

Intro

|C | | | | | | | | |

|F | | | |C | | | | |

|G | | |F | | |C | | | |

Verse 1

||C |
Well, come on, pretty baby, won't ya walk with me?

       | |
Come on, pretty baby, won't ya talk with me?

    | | | N.C.
Come on, pretty baby, give me one more chance,

          |
Try and save our romance.

          |F | |
Slow down,

        | |C | | |
Baby, now you're movin' way too fast.

        |G | |F |
You gotta gimme little lovin', gimme little lovin',

C N.C. | |C | | |
    Ow, if you want our love to last.

Verse 2

      ‖**C** | |
Well, I used to walk you home, baby, after school,

              |
Carry your books home, too.

    | | |
But now you got a boyfriend down the street,

    N.C. |
Ba - by, what you try'n' to do?

         |**F** | |
You better slow down.

       | |**C** | | |
Baby, now you're movin' way too fast.

    |**G** |**F** |
You gotta gimme little lovin', gimme little lovin',

C N.C. | |**C** | | | ‖
  Ow, if you want our love to last.

Guitar Solo   *Repeat Intro*

Verse 3

      ‖**C** | |
Well, you know that I love you; tell the world I do.

    | |
Come on, pretty baby, why can't you be true?

    | |
I need your body, baby, oh so bad.

    | **N.C.** |
The best little woman I ever had.

      |**F** | |
Slow down,

       | |**C** | | |
Baby, now you're movin' way too fast.

    |**G** |**F** |
You gotta gimme little lovin', gimme little lovin',

C N.C. | |**C** | | | ‖
  Ow, if you want our love to last.

Taxman

Words and Music by
George Harrison

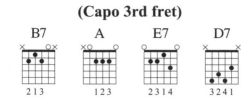

(Capo 3rd fret)

B7   A   E7   D7

Intro

| B7 |

Verse 1

‖ B7 | | |
Let me tell ___ you how it will be:
    | | | |
There's one for you, nineteen for me.
    | A |
'Cause I'm the Taxman.
    | E7 | B7 |
Yeah, I'm the Taxman.

Verse 2

‖ B7 | | |
Should five ___ percent appear too small,
    | | | |
Be thank - ful I don't take it all.
    | A |
'Cause I'm the Taxman.
    | E7 | B7 |
Yeah, I'm the Taxman.

Bridge

‖ B7 |
(If you drive a car, car.) I'll tax the street.
    | | A
(If you try to sit, sit.) I'll tax your seat.
    | B7 |
(If you get ___ too cold, cold.) I'll tax the heat.
    | | A | |
(If you take a walk, walk.) I'll tax your feet…
B7 | ‖
Taxman!

Guitar Solo |**B7** | | | | | |

                |**A**
'Cause I'm the Taxman.

           |**E7** |**B7** |
Yeah, I'm the Taxman.

Verse 3
         ‖ **B7** |
Don't ask ___ me what I want it for.

          |
(Ah, ah, Mister Wil - son!)

         | |
If you don't want to pay some more.

          |
(Ah, ah, Mister Heath!)

         |**A** |
'Cause I'm the Taxman.

         |**E7** |**B7** |
Yeah, I'm the Taxman.

Verse 4
         ‖ **B7** | |
Now my ___ advice for those who die,

        |
(Taxman!)

        | | |
Declare the pennies on your eyes.

        |
(Taxman!)

        |**A** |
'Cause I'm the Taxman.

        |**E7** |**B7**
Yeah, I'm the Taxman.

        |**D7** | ‖
And you're working for no one but…

Outro |**B7** | |
  Me.

| | | | ‖ *Fade out*

Twist and Shout

Words and Music by
Bert Russell and Phil Medley

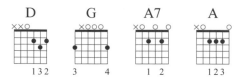

Intro |D G |A7 |D G |A7

Chorus 1
‖D   G |A7
Well, shake it up, ba - by, now, (Shake it up, ba - by.)
|D   G |A7
Twist and shout. (Twist and shout.)
                        |D   G |A7
Come on, come on, come on, come on, baby, now, (Come on, ba - by.)
                  |D G |A7
Come on and work it on out.   (Work it on out.)

Verse 1
‖D G |A7
Well, work it on out.   (Work it on out.)
            |D   G |A7
You know you look so good. (Look so good.)
            |D   G |A7
You know you got me goin', now, (Got me goin'.)
              |D   G |A7
Just like I knew you would. (Like I knew you would,   oo.)

Chorus 2   *Repeat Chorus 1*

Verse 2
                                 ‖D G |A7
You know you twist, little girl,   (Twist little girl.)
                            |D   G |A7
You know you twist so fine. (Twist so fine.)
                                    |D   G |A7
Come on and twist a little closer, now, (Twist a little closer.)
                                    |D   G |A7   ‖
And let me know that you're mine. (Let me know you're mine, oo.)

Guitar Solo   ‖:D   G |A   G |D   G |A   G :‖

                A | | |A7 | |
Interlude   Ah, ah, ah, ah, wow!

Chorus 3   *Repeat Chorus 1*

Verse 3   *Repeat Verse 2*

Outro
                                     ‖D   G |A7
Well, shake it, shake it, shake it, baby, now. (Shake it up, ba - by.)
                                    |D   G |A7
Well, shake it, shake it, shake it, baby, now. (Shake it up, ba - by.)
                                    |D   G |A7 |
Well, shake it, shake it, shake it, baby, now. (Shake it up, ba - by.)
     A | | |A7 |D ‖
Ah, ah, ah, ah.

You've Got to Hide Your Love Away

Words and Music by
John Lennon and Paul McCartney

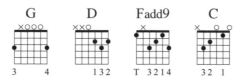

Intro | G   ‖

Verse 1
```
G     D    |Fadd9  G      |
Here I stand,  head in hand,
C               |Fadd9  C   |
Turn my face to the wall.
G     D    |Fadd9  G      |
If she's gone I can't go on,
C               |Fadd9  C  |D       ‖
Feeling two foot small.
```

Verse 2
```
G     D    |Fadd9  G      |
Every - where people    stare,
C               |Fadd9  C   |
Each and every day.
G     D    |Fadd9  G      |
I can see them laugh at me,
C               |Fadd9  C  |D      |      ‖
And I hear them say:
```

Chorus 1

```
G              |C              |D        |        |
"Hey, you've  got  to  hide  your  love  a - way!"
G              |C              |D        |        ||
"Hey, you've  got  to  hide  your  love  a - way!"
```

Verse 3

```
G        D  |Fadd9  G      |
How can I    even    try?
C           |Fadd9   C   |
I  can  never  win.
G        D  |Fadd9  G      |
Hearing them, seeing   them
C              |Fadd9  C  |D        ||
In  the  state  I'm  in.
```

Verse 4

```
G          D  |Fadd9  G      |
How could  she  say  to  me
 C              |Fadd9  C   |
"Love  will  find  a  way?"
G      D  |Fadd9  G        |
Gather 'round, all  you  clowns,
C              |Fadd9  C  |D        |        ||
Let  me  hear  you  say:
```

Chorus 2

Repeat Chorus 1

Outro

```
|G   D  |Fadd9  G    |C       |Fadd9  C      |
|G   D  |Fadd9  G    |C       |Fadd9  C   |G       ||
```

STRUM & SING

Lyrics, chord symbols, and guitar chord diagrams for your favorite songs.

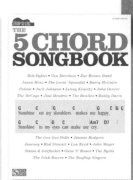

GUITAR

ADELE
00159855.................$12.99

SARA BAREILLES
00102354.................$12.99

BLUES
00159335.................$12.99

ZAC BROWN BAND
02501620.................$12.99

COLBIE CAILLAT
02501725.................$14.99

CAMPFIRE FOLK SONGS
02500686.................$12.99

CHART HITS OF 2014-2015
00142554.................$12.99

CHART HITS OF 2015-2016
00156248.................$12.99

BEST OF KENNY CHESNEY
00142457.................$14.99

KELLY CLARKSON
00146384.................$14.99

JOHN DENVER COLLECTION
02500632.................$9.95

EAGLES
00157994.................$12.99

EASY ACOUSTIC SONGS
00125478.................$14.99

50 CHILDREN'S SONGS
02500825.................$8.99

THE 5 CHORD SONGBOOK
02501718.................$12.99

FOLK SONGS
02501482.................$10.99

FOLK/ROCK FAVORITES
02501669.................$10.99

THE 4 CHORD SONGBOOK
02501533.................$12.99

THE 4-CHORD COUNTRY SONGBOOK
00114936.................$14.99

HAMILTON
00217116.................$14.99

HITS OF THE '60S
02501138.................$12.99

HITS OF THE '70S
02500871.................$9.99

HYMNS
02501125.................$8.99

JACK JOHNSON
02500858.................$16.99

ROBERT JOHNSON
00191890.................$12.99

CAROLE KING
00115243.................$10.99

BEST OF GORDON LIGHTFOOT
00139393.................$14.99

DAVE MATTHEWS BAND
02501078.................$10.95

JOHN MAYER
02501636.................$10.99

INGRID MICHAELSON
02501634.................$10.99

THE MOST REQUESTED SONGS
02501748.................$12.99

JASON MRAZ
02501452.................$14.99

PRAISE & WORSHIP
00152381.................$12.99

ELVIS PRESLEY
00198890.................$12.99

QUEEN
00218578.................$12.99

ROCK AROUND THE CLOCK
00103625.................$12.99

ROCK BALLADS
02500872.................$9.95

ED SHEERAN
00152016.................$14.99

THE 6 CHORD SONGBOOK
02502277.................$10.99

CAT STEVENS
00116827.................$14.99

TAYLOR SWIFT
00159856.................$12.99

THE 3 CHORD SONGBOOK
00211634.................$9.99

TODAY'S HITS
00119301.................$12.99

TOP CHRISTIAN HITS
00156331.................$12.99

KEITH URBAN
00118558.................$14.99

NEIL YOUNG – GREATEST HITS
00138270.................$14.99

UKULELE

THE BEATLES
00233899.................$16.99

COLBIE CAILLAT
02501731.................$10.99

JOHN DENVER
02501694.................$10.99

FOLK ROCK FAVORITES FOR UKULELE
00114600.................$9.99

THE 4-CHORD UKULELE SONGBOOK
00114331.................$14.99

JACK JOHNSON
02501702.................$17.99

JOHN MAYER
02501706.................$10.99

INGRID MICHAELSON
02501741.................$12.99

THE MOST REQUESTED SONGS
02501453.................$14.99

JASON MRAZ
02501753.................$14.99

SING-ALONG SONGS
02501710.................$15.99

Prices, content, and availability subject to change without notice.

HAL•LEONARD®

www.halleonard.com
Visit our website to see full song lists.

0418

AUTHENTIC CHORDS • ORIGINAL KEYS • COMPLETE SONGS

The *Strum It* series lets players strum the chords and sing along with their favorite hits. Each song has been selected because it can be played with regular open chords, barre chords, or other moveable chord types. Guitarists can simply play the rhythm, or play and sing along through the entire song. All songs are shown in their original keys complete with chords, strum patterns, melody and lyrics. Wherever possible, the chord voicings from the recorded versions are notated.

EASY GUITAR WITH NOTES & TAB

This series features simplified arrangements with notes, tab, chord charts, and strum and pick patterns.

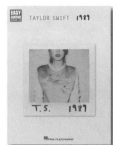

MIXED FOLIOS

00702287	Acoustic	$16.99
00702002	Acoustic Rock Hits for Easy Guitar	$14.99
00702166	All-Time Best Guitar Collection	$19.99
00699665	Beatles Best	$14.99
00702232	Best Acoustic Songs for Easy Guitar	$14.99
00119835	Best Children's Songs	$16.99
00702233	Best Hard Rock Songs	$14.99
00703055	The Big Book of Nursery Rhymes & Children's Songs	$14.99
00322179	The Big Easy Book of Classic Rock Guitar	$24.95
00698978	Big Christmas Collection	$17.99
00702394	Bluegrass Songs for Easy Guitar	$12.99
00703387	Celtic Classics	$14.99
00224808	Chart Hits of 2016-2017	$14.99
00702149	Children's Christian Songbook	$9.99
00702237	Christian Acoustic Favorites	$12.95
00702028	Christmas Classics	$8.99
00101779	Christmas Guitar	$14.99
00702185	Christmas Hits	$9.95
00702141	Classic Rock	$8.95
00702203	CMT's 100 Greatest Country Songs	$27.95
00702283	The Contemporary Christian Collection	$16.99

00702239	Country Classics for Easy Guitar	$19.99
00702282	Country Hits of 2009–2010	$14.99
00702257	Easy Acoustic Guitar Songs	$14.99
00702280	Easy Guitar Tab White Pages	$29.99
00702041	Favorite Hymns for Easy Guitar	$10.99
00140841	4-Chord Hymns for Guitar	$7.99
00702281	4 Chord Rock	$10.99
00126894	Frozen	$14.99
00702286	Glee	$16.99
00699374	Gospel Favorites	$14.95
00122138	The Grammy Awards® Record of the Year 1958-2011	$19.99
00702160	The Great American Country Songbook	$16.99
00702050	Great Classical Themes for Easy Guitar	$8.99
00702116	Greatest Hymns for Guitar	$10.99
00702130	The Groovy Years	$9.95
00702184	Guitar Instrumentals	$9.95
00148030	Halloween Guitar Songs	$14.99
00702273	Irish Songs	$12.99
00702275	Jazz Favorites for Easy Guitar	$15.99
00702274	Jazz Standards for Easy Guitar	$15.99
00702162	Jumbo Easy Guitar Songbook	$19.99
00702258	Legends of Rock	$14.99
00702261	Modern Worship Hits	$14.99

00702189	MTV's 100 Greatest Pop Songs	$24.95
00702272	1950s Rock	$15.99
00702271	1960s Rock	$15.99
00702270	1970s Rock	$15.99
00702269	1980s Rock	$15.99
00702268	1990s Rock	$15.99
00109725	Once	$14.99
00702187	Selections from O Brother Where Art Thou?	$15.99
00702178	100 Songs for Kids	$14.99
00702515	Pirates of the Caribbean	$12.99
00702125	Praise and Worship for Guitar	$10.99
00702285	Southern Rock Hits	$12.99
00121535	30 Easy Celtic Guitar Solos	$14.99
00702220	Today's Country Hits	$9.95
00121900	Today's Women of Pop & Rock	$14.99
00702294	Top Worship Hits	$15.99
00702255	VH1's 100 Greatest Hard Rock Songs	$27.99
00702175	VH1's 100 Greatest Songs of Rock and Roll	$24.95
00702253	Wicked	$12.99

ARTIST COLLECTIONS

00702267	AC/DC for Easy Guitar	$15.99
00702598	Adele for Easy Guitar	$15.99
00702040	Best of the Allman Brothers	$15.99
00702865	J.S. Bach for Easy Guitar	$14.99
00702169	Best of The Beach Boys	$12.99
00702292	The Beatles — 1	$19.99
00125796	Best of Chuck Berry	$14.99
00702201	The Essential Black Sabbath	$12.95
02501615	Zac Brown Band — The Foundation	$16.99
02501621	Zac Brown Band — You Get What You Give	$16.99
00702043	Best of Johnny Cash	$16.99
00702263	Best of Casting Crowns	$14.99
00702090	Eric Clapton's Best	$10.95
00702086	Eric Clapton — from the Album Unplugged	$10.95
00702202	The Essential Eric Clapton	$14.99
00702250	blink-182 — Greatest Hits	$15.99
00702053	Best of Patsy Cline	$14.99
00702229	The Very Best of Creedence Clearwater Revival	$15.99
00702145	Best of Jim Croce	$15.99
00702278	Crosby, Stills & Nash	$12.99
00702219	David Crowder*Band Collection	$12.95
14042809	Bob Dylan	$14.99
00702276	Fleetwood Mac — Easy Guitar Collection	$14.99
00139462	The Very Best of Grateful Dead	$15.99
00702136	Best of Merle Haggard	$12.99
00702227	Jimi Hendrix — Smash Hits	$14.99
00702288	Best of Hillsong United	$12.99
00702236	Best of Antonio Carlos Jobim	$14.99

00702245	Elton John — Greatest Hits 1970–2002	$14.99
00129855	Jack Johnson	$15.99
00702204	Robert Johnson	$10.99
00702234	Selections from Toby Keith — 35 Biggest Hits	$12.95
00702003	Kiss	$10.99
00110578	Best of Kutless	$12.99
00702216	Lynyrd Skynyrd	$15.99
00702182	The Essential Bob Marley	$12.95
00146081	Maroon 5	$14.99
00121925	Bruno Mars – Unorthodox Jukebox	$12.99
00702248	Paul McCartney — All the Best	$14.99
00702129	Songs of Sarah McLachlan	$12.95
00125484	The Best of MercyMe	$12.99
02501316	Metallica — Death Magnetic	$19.99
00702209	Steve Miller Band — Young Hearts (Greatest Hits)	$12.95
00124167	Jason Mraz	$15.99
00702096	Best of Nirvana	$15.99
00702211	The Offspring — Greatest Hits	$12.95
00138026	One Direction	$14.99
00702030	Best of Roy Orbison	$14.99
00702144	Best of Ozzy Osbourne	$14.99
00702279	Tom Petty	$12.99
00102911	Pink Floyd	$16.99
00702139	Elvis Country Favorites	$14.99
00702293	The Very Best of Prince	$15.99
00699415	Best of Queen for Guitar	$14.99
00109279	Best of R.E.M.	$14.99
00702208	Red Hot Chili Peppers — Greatest Hits	$14.99

00198960	The Rolling Stones	$16.99
00174793	The Very Best of Santana	$14.99
00702196	Best of Bob Seger	$12.95
00146046	Ed Sheeran	$14.99
00702252	Frank Sinatra — Nothing But the Best	$12.99
00702010	Best of Rod Stewart	$16.99
00702049	Best of George Strait	$14.99
00702259	Taylor Swift for Easy Guitar	$15.99
00702260	Taylor Swift — Fearless	$14.99
00139727	Taylor Swift — 1989	$17.99
00115960	Taylor Swift — Red	$16.99
00253667	Taylor Swift — Reputation	$17.99
00702290	Taylor Swift — Speak Now	$15.99
00702226	Chris Tomlin — See the Morning	$12.95
00148643	Train	$14.99
00702427	U2 — 18 Singles	$16.99
00102711	Van Halen	$16.99
00702108	Best of Stevie Ray Vaughan	$14.99
00702123	Best of Hank Williams	$14.99
00702111	Stevie Wonder — Guitar Collection	$9.95
00702228	Neil Young — Greatest Hits	$15.99
00119133	Neil Young — Harvest	$14.99
00702188	Essential ZZ Top	$10.95

Prices, contents and availability subject to change without notice.

HAL•LEONARD®

Visit Hal Leonard online at
www.halleonard.com

0418

The Band Method that Teaches Music Reading

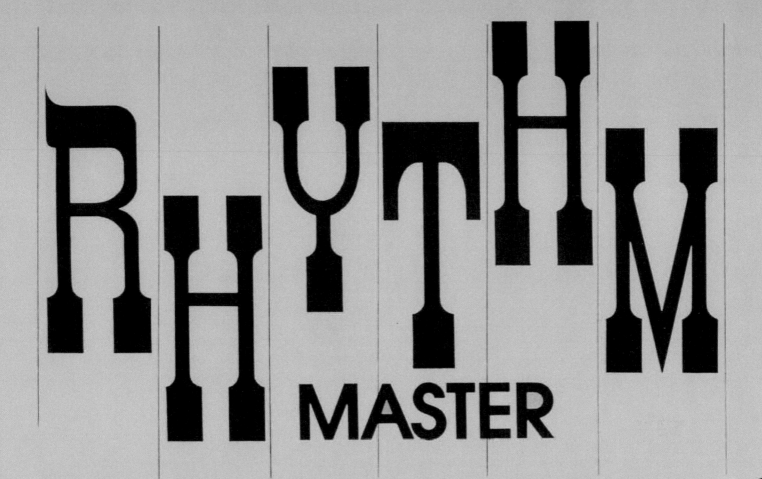

RHYTHM MASTER

BY J.R. McENTYRE AND HARRY HAINES

Southern MUSIC